Young Pathfinder 1

A CILT series for language teachers

Catching them young

Peter Satchwell and June de Silva

U

CILT

The views expressed in this book are those of the authors and do not necessarily represent the views of CILT.

Other titles in the YOUNG PATHFINDER series:

Games and fun activities (Cynthia Martin)

First published 1995
Copyright © 1995 Centre for Information on Language Teaching and Research
ISBN 1 874016 40 2

Cover by Neil Alexander
Printed in Great Britain by Bourne Press Ltd

Published by the Centre for Information on Language Teaching and Research,
20 Bedfordbury, Covent Garden, London WC2N 4LB.

Contents

Introduction

This book attempts to bring together some of the key issues which teachers and school managers will need to think about when planning to introduce (or reintroduce) a foreign language into the primary curriculum. It is aimed first and foremost at primary classroom teachers, whether in state or independent schools, whether already experienced in early teaching of modern languages (ETML) or just about to begin. Whatever your starting point, we hope the book will serve as an encouragement and as a catalyst to further thinking about aims and methodology when planning a first foreign language experience for children between the ages of four and ten. In the field of early foreign language learning (EFLL) we have come a long way in our thinking and in the quality and variety of materials available to teachers since the days of the Nuffield Primary French Project *En Avant* (1972-75), which was abandoned virtually overnight following the publication of the Burstall Report *Primary French in the Balance* (1974). Since 1990 there has been a dramatic increase in parental pressure on primary schools to introduce foreign languages at an early age. Publishers have not been slow to follow this trend, responding with an ever increasing array of materials now readily available to parents in bookshops. While much of this material is aimed at the home market rather than at schools, there has been a steady flow of French, German, Spanish and Italian resources which are eminently suited to the primary classroom. Appendix 2 gives a selection of some of the published resources that have appeared in the last five years.

Since the late 1980s there have been significant successes in ETML in the UK and Appendix 1 describes briefly most of the major local projects which have been set up since 1989. Much of the success of these ventures in EFLL derives from the enthusiasm of advisory teachers in LEAs and of individual classroom teachers who have taken a fresh look at their aims and methodology and tried to match foreign language learning activities with what they know to be successful and motivating practice in other areas of the primary curriculum.

1 Making the right start

Why start early?

Research and evidence from primary classrooms here and abroad seem to suggest that:

- children under ten are more receptive and eager to take on a new language than teenagers in secondary school;
- young children are naturally curious about language and are self-motivating;
- they absorb new language like a sponge and do not see the foreign language as a problem;
- they have no inhibitions about performing in front of others and making mistakes;
- they become personally involved in language tasks and improvise readily in the target language;
- they show empathy with foreigners and foreign cultures/customs;
- young children will readily accept 'childish' tasks, stories, songs in a foreign language;
- early foreign language learning helps children to consolidate many basic concepts in their mother tongue;
- it helps to educate both ear and tongue by enhancing sensitivity to new sound clusters, intonation patterns and rhythms;
- it teaches useful listening skills and develops learners' powers of concentration;
- it helps children to see patterns in the new language and in their own language and to draw up simple rules;
- it builds self-confidence, develops communication and social skills and raises the self-esteem of children of all abilities;
- it provides all children with a skill for life; a foundation upon which they can build later when learning any other foreign language;
- foreign language learning in primary schools can be supported and reinforced daily by the class teacher;
- teachers in primary schools have scope and flexibility to involve children in active learning and in imaginative and creative activities;
- memorable foreign language events in the school calendar, such as French breakfasts, foreign language assemblies, European weeks, parents' evenings with food served by the pupils, concerts and plays and visits abroad all provide enjoyment and boost pupils' self-confidence as well as bringing public and parental recognition to the school;
- an early start on FL1 in primary school should ultimately provide more scope for secondaries to find more time for FL2.

WHERE DO WE BEGIN?

Before embarking on a foreign language project your school will have to tackle some key organisational questions and make decisions on a number of important issues.

- Which language can we offer?
- Who will be able to teach it?
- What sort of support will the teacher(s) need? Will INSET be available?
- How long will the language experience be - one year or more?
- How will this be resourced?
- How much curriculum time will be allocated?
- How many lessons a week and how many minutes per lesson are appropriate to the age group?
- Will the FL be taught as a separate subject or will it be integrated into the normal class topic work? (This will be possible only if the class teacher is also the language teacher.)
- What help can we expect from the local secondary school, the community, the governors, the parents?
- How much planning time will be needed before we can start?
- What equipment, resources and space will be needed? How will this be funded?

If the children's first encounter with a foreign language is to be a successful one, it is vital that the teacher has planned the course, however short, well in advance. You will need to define clearly on paper what you are aiming to achieve, what you hope the learners will achieve, and what specific goals you are going to set for the learners and for yourself. You will then need to decide how you will achieve these goals by identifying appropriate pupil tasks and activities, planning your own role in the classroom, the teaching strategies you will use and the resources that will help the learners towards a sense of achievement and success. You will also need to decide how and when you will assess your own and the pupils' progress.

The lists of aims and objectives suggested here are offered as a starting point. Individual teachers will want to adapt them or add to them in the context of their own school circumstances.

AIMS

The broad aims of early foreign language learning can be set out under three main categories of development of communicative/linguistic skills, of social/cultural awareness and of learning skills, as in the following diagram:

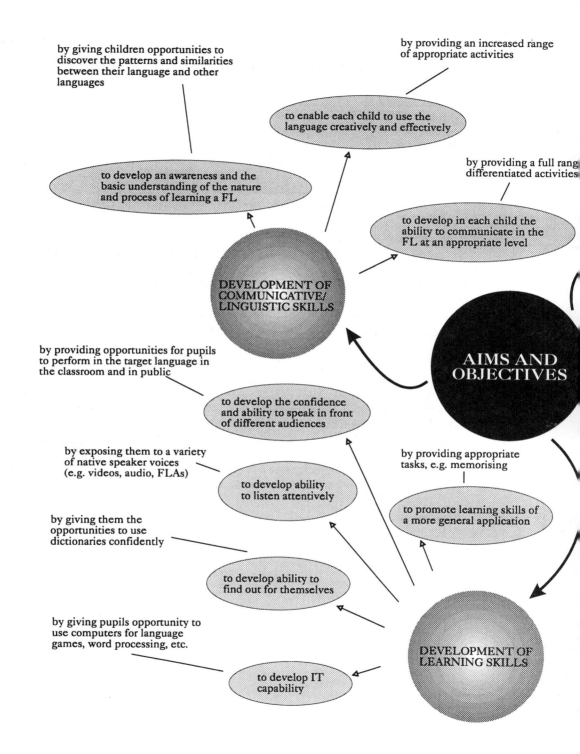

by giving children opportunities to
discover the patterns and similarities
between their language and other
languages

by providing an increased range
of appropriate activities

to enable each child to use the
language creatively and effectively

by providing a full rang
differentiated activities

to develop an awareness and the
basic understanding of the nature
and process of learning a FL

to develop in each child the
ability to communicate in the
FL at an appropriate level

DEVELOPMENT OF
COMMUNICATIVE/
LINGUISTIC SKILLS

AIMS AND
OBJECTIVES

by providing opportunities for pupils
to perform in the target language in
the classroom and in public

to develop the confidence
and ability to speak in front
of different audiences

by exposing them to a variety
of native speaker voices
(e.g. videos, audio, FLAs)

by providing appropriate
tasks, e.g. memorising

to develop ability
to listen attentively

to promote learning skills of
a more general application

by giving them the
opportunities to use
dictionaries confidently

to develop ability to
find out for themselves

by giving pupils opportunity to
use computers for language
games, word processing, etc.

DEVELOPMENT OF
LEARNING SKILLS

to develop IT
capability

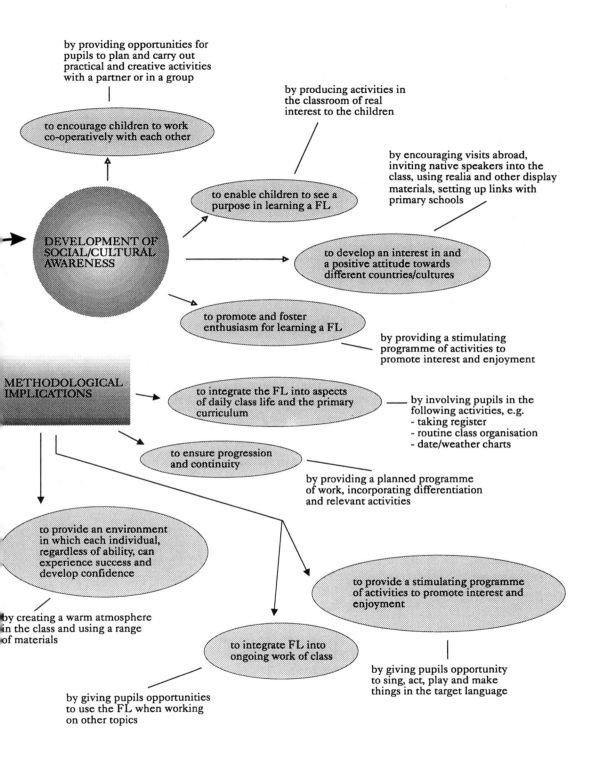

by providing opportunities for pupils to plan and carry out practical and creative activities with a partner or in a group

to encourage children to work co-operatively with each other

by producing activities in the classroom of real interest to the children

by encouraging visits abroad, inviting native speakers into the class, using realia and other display materials, setting up links with primary schools

to enable children to see a purpose in learning a FL

DEVELOPMENT OF SOCIAL/CULTURAL AWARENESS

to develop an interest in and a positive attitude towards different countries/cultures

to promote and foster enthusiasm for learning a FL

by providing a stimulating programme of activities to promote interest and enjoyment

METHODOLOGICAL IMPLICATIONS

to integrate the FL into aspects of daily class life and the primary curriculum

by involving pupils in the following activities, e.g.
- taking register
- routine class organisation
- date/weather charts

to ensure progression and continuity

by providing a planned programme of work, incorporating differentiation and relevant activities

to provide an environment in which each individual, regardless of ability, can experience success and develop confidence

to provide a stimulating programme of activities to promote interest and enjoyment

by creating a warm atmosphere in the class and using a range of materials

to integrate FL into ongoing work of class

by giving pupils opportunity to sing, act, play and make things in the target language

by giving pupils opportunities to use the FL when working on other topics

5

In order to arrive at a short list of your own specific **aims** you may have to ask yourself questions such as:

- how can I give the children an enjoyable and successful first experience of foreign language learning?
- how can I create a classroom environment which exposes them constantly to the language and the culture of the foreign country?
- how do I ensure that they have constant practice at listening to the target language?
- how do I ensure that they have understood?
- how can I ensure that they learn **in** the language and not just **about** the language?
- how do I give them maximum opportunities to use the language themselves?
- what activities can I devise to involve them in speaking to each other in the language?
- how can I include making and doing in the foreign language (e.g. menus, colouring, drawing, folding, cutting out, modelling)?
- how can I encourage empathy for and curiosity about the foreign country and people?
- what links can I make with the foreign country - school link, class correspondence, visits abroad?
- how can I ensure that children of all abilities achieve a sense of progress and success?
- what links can I make between the sounds, rhythms, intonation, stress of the target language and the mother tongue?
- how will I enhance the children's awareness of language in general?
- how will I organise my classroom and my daily routines to accommodate the new language?

OBJECTIVES

In order to realise your aims, you will need to set your own specific objectives. Those set out below have been gleaned from several primary teachers over a number of years:

- to involve pupils in active learning
  through games, role-play, mime, pairwork, action songs, making and doing;
- to develop confidence in listening skills and the ability to listen attentively
  through a progressive re-education of the ear to hear new sounds, vowel and consonant clusters, rhythms and intonation;
- to develop a sense of fun, but also real accuracy in speaking skills by providing intensive practice and repetition
  through rhymes, comptines, tongue-twisters, songs, chants, raps;
- to help children progressively to match sounds to the printed word
  by encouraging from an early stage simple labelling, word and picture matching;

- to provide the learners with a real sense of achievement
  by building in regular short-term goals (performance tasks): simple graded objectives in speaking and listening which are easily accessible to all;
- to develop the learners' self-confidence in speaking the new language
  by encouraging them to use it at every opportunity in class and out - to their classmates, their teacher, the headteacher, visitors, parents and in public performances;
- to develop the children's ability to find out new words and facts for themselves
  by reference to dictionaries, reference books, other adults, IT;
- to provide constant revision and reinforcement opportunities for children of all abilities
  through regular use of IT and other media: computer software, concept keyboard, video and audio cassettes, language master, board and card games, school links abroad, penfriend correspondence;
- to create a classroom and whole-school environment where the use of the foreign language for normal everyday communication is obviously valued
  through use of bilingual labelling around the school, display in corridors, performance in assemblies, school concerts, parents' open days, etc.

CHOOSING YOUR TOPICS

Identify a limited number of broad topics; find the resources; create pupil activities; plan a notional timescale for each topic.

Possible topics (these are common to most primary FL schemes in the UK, Canada and Australia)

ME

greetings
name, age, family, relationships
where I live, address, nationality
my body
clothes I wear + seasons, temperatures, weather + colours
meals + likes/dislikes, favourites
animals/pets + colour, age + food likes
numbers, counting songs/rhymes/games + mental arithmetic + time

OUR TOWN/ VILLAGE

my house/street + neighbourhood
local shops + shopping + prices /money
leisure activities/sports/hobbies
holidays + seasons + national festivals, e.g. Easter + decorated eggs, Christmas
communications

THE WIDER WORLD/ THE ENVIRONMENT

people who help us/ people and their work
water, rivers, ponds, the sea
trees, woods, leaves, fruits
farming + animals
insects + plants + life-cycle, habitat, food-chain
flight, space
food tasting + cooking, baking + simple recipes, menus
UK and its European neighbours
short first visit to France/Belgium/Germany/Spain

PLANNING THE TIMESCALE

Having identified four or five broad topics for the year, you will need to find appropriate resources for the age group and plot a notional timescale, including in your planning a grid/flowchart of the specific language items and the pupil tasks and activities you hope to cover each week. An initial planning sheet might be set out in a flowchart like the one on pp 10-11 or it might be in grid format as in the example below:

Week	Lesson	Pupil tasks	Language items	Resources
1	1	Learn parts of body	*la tête, bouche, oreille, jambe, main* *le nez, cou, bras, doigt* *les pieds, oreilles*	OHT of body Skeleton Aerobics (cassette)
		Play *Jacques a dit: Touchez la...!* Label parts of body Sing Head + shoulders, knees and toes in FL Make/colour string puppet		Song cassette Card/scissors crayons
3	7	Learn clothes vocabulary	*un pull, pantalon, chapeau* *une jupe, robe, chemise* *des chaussures, chaussettes*	Box of clothes to try on Colour chart
5	12	Describe self + others Artwork, collages	*je suis grand(e), petit(e) mince, gros(se)* *j'ai les yeux bleus, les cheveux longs, etc.* *je/il/elle porte une jupe verte/un pantalon noir*	IT: *Quelle tête*
6	15	Mini fashion show + pupil script Class dress up, perform to school/parents	*Julie porte un beau chemisier blanc et une jupe bleue, etc.*	Micro/PA

FINDING APPROPRIATE RESOURCES

Having researched what is available in terms of ready-made commercially produced materials, you will then have to go out and beg, borrow or buy what you need. But it is worth remembering that some of the best resources are those that teachers have made themselves, adapting ideas from here, there and everywhere. Many foreign language activities for the youngest children (four to seven) can be adaptations of well-known primary class materials in the mother tongue - or they can be nursery/primary booklets (often labelled *Maternelle* in France) bought in France/Germany/Italy/Spain specifically designed for pre-school children to learn from at home.

For older children of eight years upwards it will become progressively easier to use commercially published materials designed for the classroom, but you should be aware of the dangers of taking a secondary-style 'coursebook' approach in a primary school. You will probably try to acquire a little of everything initially in order to build up a flexible and varied stock of pupil materials. This will inevitably take a number of years, depending on your school's budget.

However, even some of the most delightful and professionally produced materials such as *Farandole, Kangourou, Aventures, Le petit Trampoline, Trampoline 1 + 2, Le français en chantant* , or *Du und ich* and *Wer? Wie? Was?* will need careful study by the teacher and often radical adaptation or abbreviation in order to match the needs of a particular class in the UK.

You will need to be critical and courageous in 'picking out the plums' from materials produced in France or Germany, as many of them presuppose a much more generous timescale for foreign language learning and a more bookbound, teacher-centred style of primary teaching than is customary in most British schools.

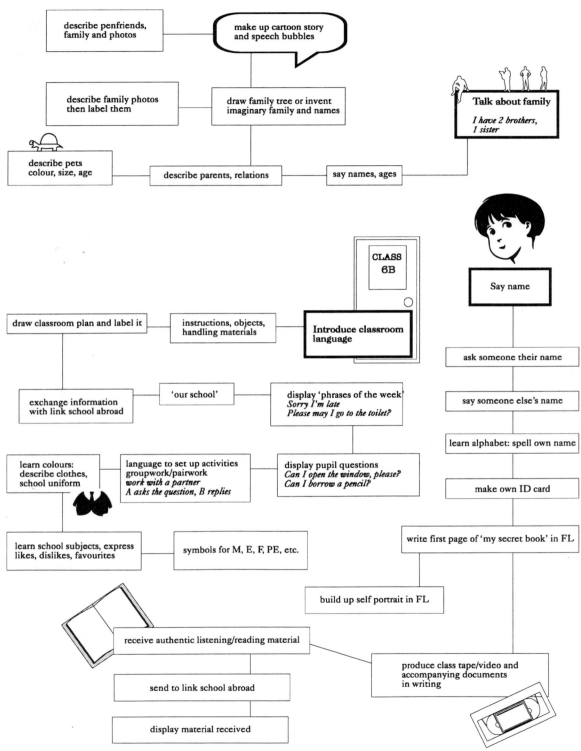

describe penfriends, family and photos

make up cartoon story and speech bubbles

describe family photos then label them

draw family tree or invent imaginary family and names

Talk about family
*I have 2 brothers,
1 sister*

describe pets colour, size, age

describe parents, relations

say names, ages

CLASS 6B

Introduce classroom language

Say name

draw classroom plan and label it

instructions, objects, handling materials

ask someone their name

say someone else's name

exchange information with link school abroad

'our school'

display 'phrases of the week'
*Sorry I'm late
Please may I go to the toilet?*

learn alphabet: spell own name

learn colours: describe clothes, school uniform

language to set up activities groupwork/pairwork
*work with a partner
A asks the question, B replies*

display pupil questions
*Can I open the window, please?
Can I borrow a pencil?*

make own ID card

learn school subjects, express likes, dislikes, favourites

symbols for M, E, F, PE, etc.

write first page of 'my secret book' in FL

build up self portrait in FL

receive authentic listening/reading material

produce class tape/video and accompanying documents in writing

send to link school abroad

display material received

10

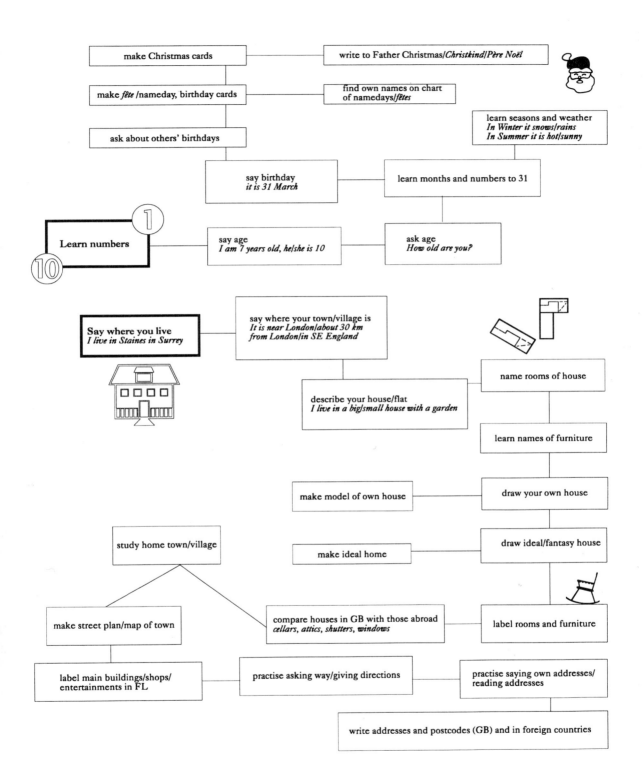

make Christmas cards — write to Father Christmas/*Christkind*/*Père Noël*

make *fête*/nameday, birthday cards — find own names on chart of namedays/*fêtes*

learn seasons and weather
In Winter it snows/rains
In Summer it is hot/sunny

ask about others' birthdays

say birthday
it is 31 March — learn months and numbers to 31

Learn numbers

say age
I am 7 years old, he/she is 10 — ask age
How old are you?

Say where you live
I live in Staines in Surrey — say where your town/village is
It is near London/about 30 km from London/in SE England

name rooms of house

describe your house/flat
I live in a big/small house with a garden

learn names of furniture

make model of own house — draw your own house

study home town/village

make ideal home — draw ideal/fantasy house

make street plan/map of town

compare houses in GB with those abroad
cellars, attics, shutters, windows — label rooms and furniture

label main buildings/shops/entertainments in FL — practise asking way/giving directions — practise saying own addresses/reading addresses

write addresses and postcodes (GB) and in foreign countries

11

EMBEDDING THE FOREIGN LANGUAGE IN THE SCHOOL CURRICULUM

Whatever the topic or the time allocations, you will inevitably run out of time in your discrete 20- or 30-minute sessions. If you are not the class teacher, you will have to think how you can enlist the aid of your colleagues, to help reinforce elements of the foreign language in their classroom routines throughout the school week. For example, most primary school teachers, with a little encouragement, will be prepared to carry out small routine tasks in French, German, Spanish or Italian if coached in the basic vocabulary. Class teachers **can:**

- call the register/get the class to number off
- take the dinner money
- line the children up
- give basic classroom instructions
- do quick mental arithmetic for fun
- take PE, aerobics, games in the playground
- practice foreign songs
- help children create bilingual displays,
- make collages, puppets, masks, etc...

Slowly, the foreign language can be embedded in the primary curriculum and begin to permeate the week's activities if other teachers join in in a modest way. The overwhelming evidence from Scottish, English and Irish primary schools where this approach has been followed is that the whole staff usually gets bitten by the bug and wants to join in the fun, especially when children are encouraged to show off their language skills in school performances of songs, rhymes, playlets, or fashion shows, for example.

If the teacher can involve parents or other language speaking adults in the school community, so much the better. Primary teachers should not be timid in asking for linguistic and practical help from their language teacher colleagues of the secondary school next door, either through the loan of their Foreign Language Assistant or a member of staff to do some team-teaching or to lend support in organising a foreign language day/evening /week in the Summer term!

In time, it will become clear how some areas of the primary curriculum can easily be taught through the foreign language, and ideas for collaborative teaching will develop. Many examples of good practice from primary schools all over Scotland are contained in the SOED videos pack *Foreign languages in the primary school* (SCOPE, 1994) and readers will also find several detailed case studies written by primary teachers in Scotland and the South of England in the forthcoming book: *Reflections on Practice 2: Teaching foreign languages to young learners* (CILT, 1995).

2   Planning for progression

It is important that the children feel that they are making progress linguistically and that they can **do** things with the foreign language, i.e. have fun, play games, talk about things which interest them, communicate with others, take part in performances, gain access to information through the foreign language. But lessons need to go beyond the purely linguistic and should, ideally, reinforce all the other skills that children are developing elsewhere in the curriculum.

It will be clear to teachers who are introducing a language to five- or six-year-olds that the emphasis for them will need to be on **Listening** and **Speaking**, with only limited reading recognition of key words and short phrases. Children of this age will need extensive exposure to listening before they will gradually acquire the confidence to speak - all in their own time. But songs, rhymes and games will automatically lead to display, labels, mobiles, models and occasional worksheets with very simple instructions in the target language, e.g.   *Colorie le poisson - en rouge, vert et jaune.*
*Zeichne einen **großen** Schneemann und zwei **kleine** Schneemänner. Schneide sie aus.*

Progression in the four language skills can be represented in a number of ways, depending on the age and ability of the learners. We hope teachers will find the following diagrams useful when they are planning their own pathways. For the sake of clarity, each skill is treated separately, but in the classroom most tasks will inevitably involve more than one skill: e.g. Listen and Draw, Listen and Write, Read and Speak, Listen and Draw and Label, etc.

Listening and speaking

Over a series of lessons the learning process will often progress along these lines:

	——— Teacher ———	——— Pupils ———
A	Teacher presents new language	Pupil receptive phase
B	Teacher controls practice of new language	Pupil acquisition phase - pupil practice
C	Teacher provides opportunities to use new language creatively	Pupil performance phase - pupil use of new language for their own purposes

LISTENING

Pupils will need to listen to: the teacher
each other
audio/video cassettes
native speakers in the classroom and outside
e.g. parents, Foreign Language Assistants, foreign
    visitors from abroad.

A - Teacher presentation

Teacher presents :

• visuals/Flashcards/OHP symbols +
  single words
• short phrases/ single sentences
• question + answer T/P
• question + answer P/P

Maximum support from
teacher through gesture,
mime, body language.
Controlled, limited
structures and lexis.

B - Pupil practice

The same foreign language items presented in a broader
context: familiar language spoken on video/audio cassette by
native speakers.

Pupils listen for   one key word (e.g. name/age/place)
    gist (e.g. what is going on? where? when?)
    specific details (e.g. time, cost, directions)

Pupils have to spot the familiar from a context of relatively
straightforward unfamiliar language: short and accessible
items; still supported by prompts from teacher.

C - Pupil use

Authentic, relatively unscripted native speakers on audio/video cassette.

Pupils listen for gist
    specifics (three or more answers)
  listen to longer, more challenging texts in a variety of situations

Pupils are challenged to pick out the familiar from more complex authentic
speech, full of unpredictables (as in real life situations in a foreign country).

SPEAKING

Pupils will need to speak to: the teacher(s)
each other
other adults (headteacher, governors, parents, visitors)
native speakers (from town or school twinning, FLA).

A - Presentation

Teacher presents visuals/Flashcards + single words.

    Pupils repeat in chorus/groups/individually
    Pupils repeat short phrases (pronunciation + intonation!)
    Pupils repeat whole phrases/sentences, questions + answers.

Maximum support from teacher; concentration on accurate mimicry, pronunciation, intonation.

B - Pupil practice

T/P dialogues as model.

Pairwork/groupwork:
* P/P dialogues **with** visual cues
* P/P dialogues **without** visual cues
* P/T dialogues **without** cues
* P/P performance in private (pairs/groups)

Constant support and monitoring by teacher

C - Pupil use

T/P questions (more complex)

P/T questions (pupils need to practise **asking** the questions!)

Pupils begin to
    use coping language
    initiate conversations
    sustain conversations
    transfer language from one context to another
    manipulate language to create new dialogues in new situations
    perform playlets, songs, raps, rhymes in public
    manipulate language in real life conversations

At this stage the teacher provides opportunities for pupils to work independently of her and to be creative in the target language.

It is obvious that not all pupils will reach the latter stages of this sequence, but some do, well before the end of their primary school days, and we should give the more gifted children every opportunity to perform at this level; if we encourage them to take the initiative in the foreign language they will often surprise us!

READING

Reading skills can, and probably should, be developed simultaneously with speaking skills, but at a slower pace, and always **after** intensive listening and speaking practice. Many teachers of French in particular know the pitfalls of introducing the printed form of the language too early and the dire mispronunciations that can result, but with careful planning and selection of texts children will benefit enormously from being encouraged to read simple stories and cartoons for their own pleasure.

We should aim to progress
from
single words (labels, names, signs)
through
short phrases (instructions, dates, captions)
simple sentences
simple questions
simple dialogue (speech bubbles)
simple captions/narrative
familiar stories (fairy tales, well-known children's stories in translation)
unfamiliar stories (cartoons, picture strip)

Reading progression will be more variable and harder to define than progress in listening and speaking, but older juniors of nine and ten have proved well capable of coping with, and enjoying, a colour-coded, graded reading programme in the foreign language such as *Bibliobus*, Box A and A+, and *Lesekiste*, Box A, from MGP.

WRITING

Most forms of writing in a foreign language at primary level will be confined to copywriting tasks. These are, however, valuable to pupils of all abilities as a reinforcement activity. The experience of several schools suggests that children gain real satisfaction from having written some of the key vocabulary and that writing in the foreign language can even prove more successful for some of the less able pupils than writing in their mother tongue (no previous experience of failure!).

A possible progression might be:

- copy single words;
- label pictures;
- write single words from memory;
- copy short phrases with support;
- write simple speech bubbles with support from memory;
- write simple books, cartoon stories for younger pupils to read;
- from a model: write own rhymes, poems, raps;
- from authentic models: create own slogans, adverts, posters for display;
- word process own texts, redraft with teacher help for display;
- word process bilingual signs and notices in large print for display round the school.

MEASURING PROGRESS

It is clear that teachers will need to build into their planning chart some form of continuous assessment of pupils' progress. This could take the form of regular waystages or short-term goals through which the teacher can monitor individual progress and the pupils can prove to themselves that they really can do things in the foreign language. These goals could be **easy performance tasks** which are **fun** for the pupils and **arise naturally out of the learning process.** There is certainly no need for formal pencil and paper tests in primary school language classes!

In most cases the tasks can be oral role-play situations based round an already familiar scenario. If children are encouraged to dress up for their part and bring in props, so much the better. The class can then be encouraged to join in the teacher's assessment process by being a critical audience and awarding points for good performances. For example, a class that has just worked for four or five weeks on 'My house' might well be asked to make a model or drawing of their real or fantasy house and to describe orally the furnishing of each room. A class that has worked on 'Leisure and hobbies' might be asked to perform short dialogues or TV-style interviews in pairs expressing their likes/dislikes, favourite sports and pastimes. These could be recorded on audio or video cassette and evaluated by the whole class.

In order to produce a continuous assessment profile of each child you may find it easiest to keep records on a very simple scale from 0-2 where:
0 = task not achieved; 1 = task partly achieved; 2 = task fully achieved.
At infant level it would suffice to record informally progress in Listening and Speaking skills only. In the junior school you may wish to add some reading and simple copywriting tasks to the profile. And pupils' progress in the non-linguistic skills could also be added, if necessary.

With infants a very simple self-assessment sheet could be produced like one which was devised by a class teacher of a Surrey First School for her own class of six- and seven-year-olds. It was basically a list of 'I can...' statements which the children completed with enthusiasm during their first year of French. You will no doubt think of other variations on the theme.

In addition to assessment tasks two or three times a term, it is also motivating for all children - and especially for the less able learners - if the teacher has a constant stock of tiny **rewards** up her sleeve for an extra special effort in class. For example, one firm (*Buttons à la Mode*) produces small merit badges with faces and slogans in several languages. The teacher could stock up in European supermarkets with strips of cheap fruit-flavoured sweets in coloured wrappers which are always popular with small children and add a flavour of authenticity to the lesson. Similarly, primary teachers have brought back from abroad cheap pencils, rubbers, sharpeners, rulers, stickers, notebooks, etc. - all of which add a foreign ambience to the classroom and make excellent prizes for language games.

The important principle is not testing the pupils, but motivating them! Once children have experienced success in using the language, they will want to learn more - and then there is no stopping them! And the ultimate goal for all young learners should be their first visit abroad to try out the language which they have learnt in class for real - whether it is a day trip to France or several days in a centre further afield, if it can possibly be arranged. Such trips offer enormous potential for cross-curricular activities and provide a stimulus for work back in the classroom for weeks afterwards - but that is the theme for another book in this series!

ENSURING PROGRESSION FROM PRIMARY TO SECONDARY

When pupils have been learning a language in year 5 and/or 6, it is important that the secondary school(s) in the area is fully aware of the work that has been done in your school and that some record of pupils' achievement is passed on to the secondary languages department. Ideally, this record should identify in simple terms the pupils' competence in Listening , Speaking and Reading and should be accompanied by a clear account of the topics and language areas covered by the whole class. Only if secondary schools are fully informed about the children's foreign language experience - and have been invited to come and see for themselves what your children can do! - is there any real chance that they will then build on the foundations laid in the primary school and not demotivate your pupils at the age of eleven by going back to the beginning again.

Where liaison between primary and secondary schools is taken seriously and professionally, exciting reciprocal visits and staff collaboration over the organisation of foreign language competitions and events can ensure that teachers in both phases visit each other regularly during the year and are thus fully aware of each other's approaches and practices. Many schools in Sussex, for example, build carefully in year 7 upon the *Salut* materials that have been used in year 6 of their primary schools. This provides security and continuity for the new pupils and a basis for consolidation in the first term of the secondary school. In some areas of Surrey, secondary languages departments work closely with their primary colleagues to organise annual French days and 'teach-ins', where year 7 and 8 pupils teach primary pupils a particular topic for the day. There are infinite possibilities for such cross-phase collaboration if teachers give such initiatives a high profile and negotiate the time with their headteachers and their colleagues.

DEVELOPING OTHER LEARNING SKILLS

As mentioned above, the learning of a foreign language should not be seen as a purely linguistic exercise for the children. Good language lessons will inevitably have positive spin-offs in reinforcing and developing skills that pupils are learning and using in other areas of the curriculum. They will also be broadening their awareness of language in all its facets. We have listed below some of the skills that can easily be learnt and used in primary foreign language lessons. You will think of others to extend the list.

Learning a foreign language can reinforce:

- mathematical skills: mental arithmetic, class surveys - block graphs, pie charts, dates, 24 hour clock, length, area, shapes
- pencil skills: complete drawing, colour/shade in
- artistic skills: draw/paint, collages, posters, adverts; cut out/fold, make models (shops, village, houses), make puppets
- book making: write stories and make cartoon books for younger children to read
- reference skills: learn to use picture dictionaries, bilingual dictionaries, reference books
- ball skills: playground ball games and physical skills in games like *Twister*
- music and movement: rehearse songs, dance, aerobics, PE activities
- IT skills: word processing (*European Folio, Write on, Prompt Writer*);
  games (*6 French/German/Spanish Games, Kidnap, L'aventure*);
  text manipulation (*Fun with texts, Developing Tray, Expose*);
  work with a concept keyboard (*Touch Explorer Plus, Eauthun, Intro Tray Concept*).

3   Methods and activities that work - good practice

'One of the most characteristic features of good teaching and learning is the sense of enjoyment and motivation which is created.' (*Modern Foreign Languages for ages 11 to 16*, NC Working Group, October 1990). Although this is a statement from a document focused on secondary school pupils, there is no doubt that it applies equally to primary children.

If one of the main aims of teaching a foreign language to young learners is 'to give children an enjoyable and successful first experience', how is this realised by ensuring effective teaching and learning? What is good practice in early foreign language learning? Many of the points that follow are characteristic of good primary practice in any curriculum area, few are solely applicable to learning a foreign language.

- Pupils are given opportunities to work in pairs and groups.
- Pupils are given clear instructions.
- A supportive atmosphere is provided, in which pupils are not afraid to try again and in which they feel able to 'fail in safety'.
- A range of teaching strategies are used including music, role-play and drama, thereby encouraging active participation by the pupils.
- The pace is appropriate with plenty of opportunities for repetition and practice, but in as many different ways as possible to avoid any possibility of boredom.
- The use of extensive visual stimuli, as well as objects to handle and make.
- The provision of extensive support to aid pupil understanding, including the use of visuals, mime and gesture.
- A variety of activities are provided involving the use of rhymes, poems, games and puzzles.

GAMES

One of the main objectives outlined in Chapter 2 was 'to involve pupils in active learning'. One of the most effective ways of doing this is through games.

Games provide an excellent means of practising, repeating and reinforcing new vocabulary and structures in all four skill areas, Listening, Speaking, Reading and Writing, as well as helping to maintain the interest of the pupils. They also give many opportunities for pair and group work, are generally greatly enjoyed by pupils and therefore help to promote positive attitudes in the classroom. It is not possible to give details of all the games that can be played in the foreign language as these could fill a book themselves (*Young Pathfinder 2: Games and fun activities*, CILT, 1995). However, many games that are already very well known to the pupils in their mother tongue lend themselves extremely well to being played in the foreign language. These include:

- Snap
- Dominoes
- Pairs or Pelmanism
- Battleships
- Happy Families
- Loto

- Blockbusters
- Simon says
- Hangman
- Beetle
- Kim's game
- Noughts and crosses

Flashcard Games

As well as being very useful for introducing new language, flashcards are an excellent means of practising vocabulary and structures. They can be purchased from commercial publishers or you can make your own by using drawings, photographs or pictures cut out from magazines. There are many games that can be played using flash cards, such as:

- **Guess the card.** Having introduced a number of vocabulary items, the teacher selects and 'hides' one card. The pupils have to guess which one it is. The successful pupil takes the place of the teacher.

- **Repeat if it is true.** Using the cards as a stimulus, the teacher says a word or phrase, and the pupils repeat it. When they are sufficiently confident they are asked to repeat after the teacher only if they are given the correct word or phrase. The speed of the game can be increased to make it more exciting and the pupils enjoy trying to 'beat' the teacher.

- **Noughts and crosses.** The aims of playing noughts and crosses, in French for example, would be to repeat and practise new vocabulary and to practise the structure *C'est un/une...*

The materials needed are a board or an OHP.

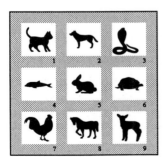

A nine square grid is drawn with the numbers 1 to 9 written in the spaces. The appropriate flashcards are stuck into the squares and the class is divided into two teams of noughts or crosses. One member of the team selects a number and answers the question *Qu'est-ce que c'est?* If s/he is correct, the flashcard is removed and replaced by a nought or a cross. The winner is the first team to get three in a row.

Number games

There are many good games for practising numbers.

- **Loto.** Loto cards can be made beforehand and counters provided, or the pupils can write down a selection of numbers and cross them out as they are called, either by the teacher or another member of the class. The winner must have their cards 'checked' by calling the numbers back in French.

- **Effacez!** The class is divided into two teams and a selection of numbers to be practised is written on the board in a random fashion. One member of each team comes to the board and a number is called out by the teacher. The first team member to rub out the correct number gains a point for their team. Pupils can also take the teacher's role and call out the numbers. Other versions of this game involve having numbers written on the board which have to be circled according to the teacher's instructions or having a blank board and pupils have to write the number that has been called out.

- **Plouf!** The numbers which are to be practised are written on the board in the form of stepping stones across a river. To safely cross the river, the numbers have to be said correctly. If an error is made the pupil falls in the water.

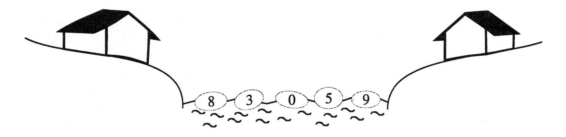

Card games

As well as the motivation and enjoyment that arises from practising language through games with cards, there is also the possibility of involving pupils in making their own sets of cards.

- **Pairs or pelmanism.** The objective is to win pairs of cards by matching a word or phrase with a picture. The cards are laid face down on the table and pupils take it in turns to pick up two cards at a time. As they do so, they must name the picture or read the phrase out loud. If they make a pair, they keep the cards. The winner is the person who has most cards.

- **Dominoes.** Again, the domino cards may be provided by the teacher or made by the children. They can be used to practise numbers, or to practise vocabulary by matching a picture to a word or a picture to a picture. The game is played in the same way as traditional dominoes with the objective of getting rid of all your dominoes.

Memory games

Memory games are generally popular and give the pupil a real reason for recalling something they have learned.

- **Kim's game.** There are several versions of this game which can be played using real objects, OHP visuals or flashcards. A collection of objects is shown to the pupils. The teacher names them and the class repeats. The objects are then removed or covered and the pupils have to name what was there. Alternatively, one object is removed and the pupils have to identify the missing item.

- **I went to market and I bought...** The teacher or a pupil begins with a set phrase which must be completed with a noun. The next person repeats what was said before but with the addition of their own noun. Supportive miming is allowed!

Guessing games

- **What is in the box/bag?** At the simplest level this involves guessing individual objects and naming them, but at a higher level the pupils can ask questions to help identify the item. A 'feely bag' can be used to give another version of this game.

- **Hangman.** This is a means of practising the alphabet in the foreign language and follows the same rules as the traditional game. It can be played in pairs, groups or as a whole class activity with teams. The game can be of a general nature or focused on one particular vocabulary area.

- **Hide and seek.** Hide a small object somewhere in the classroom and pupils have to guess where it is hidden. This is very useful for practising prepositions and the children can be encouraged by being told if they are 'hot' or 'cold' depending on how accurate their guess is.

SONGS

Apart from straightforward enjoyment, singing in the foreign language gives pupils an excellent opportunity to practise structures, intonation and pronunciation. Songs may also include movement and actions and can be presented and exploited in many ways:

- If possible, introduce a song by setting the scene - this provides the context.

- Present the song with visuals, either using flashcards, drawings or realia.

- Include appropriate actions or gestures. Body language has a very important role to play in communicating meaning.

- Keep the written text of the song until the pupils are familiar with the pronunciation and intonation of the verses.

- Songs may be used for active listening comprehension. Pupils can be given copies of the text with certain words omitted. While listening to a taped recording of the song, the pupils must try to fill in the blanks. Support can be made available by having the missing words written on the board or at the bottom of the words sheet. This activity lends itself very well to pair or small group work.

- A similar cloze type activity is to ask the children to replace certain words in the song with illustrations.

- Pupils enjoy producing their own versions of well known songs by adding another verse or changing some of the words.

- When the pupils are confident with the written text, they are often eager to copy down the songs for future reference and to illustrate them. This in itself is a means of showing understanding of the song's content.

- There are many topics which are enhanced by the use of songs. If working on the theme of the body, for example, the French songs *Alouette* and *Savez - vous planter les choux* are ideal for practising the appropriate vocabulary.

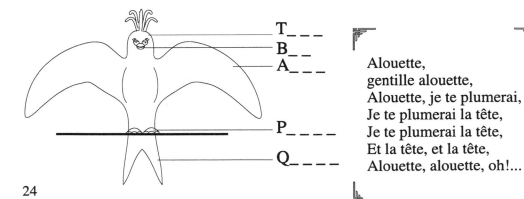

T_ _ _
B_ _
A_ _ _

P_ _ _ _

Q_ _ _ _

Alouette,
gentille alouette,
Alouette, je te plumerai,
Je te plumerai la tête,
Je te plumerai la tête,
Et la tête, et la tête,
Alouette, alouette, oh!...

RHYMES, RHYTHM AND RAPS

Simple poems, nonsense rhymes and *comptines* are all enjoyed by pupils, as well as being an excellent vehicle for practising intonation in a painless way.

If one takes a simple *comptine*, for example:

Dans le pré... et dans la mare

En courant dans le pré
J'ai rencontré un bélier

En regardant là-haut
J'ai aperçu un oiseau

En passant
près de la mare
J'ai vu un canard

En traversant le jardin
J'ai croisé un lapin

Although the language may appear to be quite complex with the inclusion of a past tense, the short rhyming couplets are, generally, easy to introduce with plenty of gesture and appropriate flashcards. Many children have a natural sense of rhythm and are able to produce a rap based on a traditional *comptine* - often more effectively than their teacher.

The next step is to help pupils produce their own original poetry. This is not as daunting as it may at first appear and usually brings extremely satisfying results. One starting point is to take known items of vocabulary and find words which rhyme with them.

> *un crayon   un garçon*
> *mon frère   ma mère*
> *noir   au revoir*
> *un avion   un camion*
> *Bonne fête   Hugette*
> *il fait beau   bravo*
> *une pomme   une gomme*

Poems need be only simple two-line rhyming couplets. These can be worked out in pairs or groups and then put together, if appropriate, into a class poem. The theme of animals could produce:

J'ai un chat
Il n'aime pas les rats!

Mon ami a un chien
Il est toujours bien

Ma soeur adore les souris
Parce qu'elles sont très gentilles

Mon professeur a un cheval noir
C'est tout. Au revoir!

Je m'appelle
YvettE
j'Ai
oNze ans

Bonjour!
Olivier
Nathalie
Jérôme
Odette
JacqUes
Au Revoir!

Mein
Onkel
wohNt
nichT
Am
Grossglockner

Of course, poetry does not have to rhyme and ideas for producing shape poems and acrostic poems, for example, can be found in many primary school poetry books.

DRAMA-BASED ACTIVITIES

The value in using drama-based activities lies in what they bring out in the pupils in the process. They do not necessarily have to lead to a major performance in front of a large audience. There may be no audience in mind other than the children taking part themselves. Of course, one pair or group may wish to share their performance with another pair or group or even the whole class, if the teacher feels it is appropriate.

Any dialogue or role-play can be treated as drama. Younger pupils usually enjoy taking on another character, whether it is someone well known or imaginary. After all, there are only so many ways to practise introducing yourself in the foreign language, especially to fellow classmates who know only too well your name, age and where you live! However, take on the persona of someone else - a famous footballer, a pop star or an alien from another planet, and the whole exercise becomes more fun and motivating. The introduction of props and costumes leads to even greater enjoyment and enthusiasm. A fashion show with *compère*, cat walk and appropriate music has been known to persuade the most reluctant linguist to contribute, and what a practical and lively way to rehearse introductions, clothes and colours vocabulary!

26

Drama-based techniques for early language learners include:

- The use of a ball or soft toy to initiate language. For example, the teacher asks a question of the class and throws the soft ball to a specific pupil to initiate the response.

- **The name game**. Pupils take it in turns to introduce themselves by giving a noun that begins with the same letter as their name. '*Hello! I am Peter the pear.*' '*Hello! I am June the jaguar.*' This can be extended by asking pupils to present the person on their left to the rest of the group.

- **Getting into groups**. This is a useful way to practise numbers by giving the instruction '*Get into groups of three, five...*' and so on.

- A similar technique is to seat the pupils in a circle and allocate a number to each pupil, so that there are several ones, twos, threes or fours. One pupil stands in the middle of the circle and the teacher calls out a number so that all the pupils with that number must stand up and change places. The pupil in the middle must also try to find a seat. The pupil left without a chair now takes over the place in the middle of the circle. This game can be used to practise different types of vocabulary, e.g. the alphabet, animals, months etc.

- **Fruit salad**. Pupils are given the name of a fruit; four or five different ones works well. The leader calls out 'lemons' and all the lemons change places. If 'fruit salad' is called everyone changes. This can also be played with chairs and with the added excitement of removing one chair after each go!

- **Party game**. The setting for this could be at a party, a picnic or in a café. The pupils are told to imagine they are holding something to eat and/or something to drink. They are then asked to circulate, greet people, and to find out what three other 'guests' are eating or drinking. At the end of the game they stand in a circle and one person is elected to stand in the middle. The rest of the group have to try to remember and say what that person was drinking and eating.

- **Taking on a character**. This can be imaginary, for example an alien, or someone well known. There are only so many ways to practise certain structures and vocabulary, especially in the early stages of foreign language learning and therefore taking on another personality can bring authenticity and interest to rehearsing '*What is your name?*' and similar phrases.

- **Using props**. These can be provided by the teacher or brought by the pupils. A telephone can be used in many ways, e.g. to practise numbers, for role-plays or in a game such as *Pass the phone*. This is a type of *Pass the parcel* in which the pupils pass the telephone until it rings (simulated by the teacher). The pupil who has the phone speaks according to the task set or the question asked by the teacher.

- **Miming**. This can be done by the whole class or individually. Group miming is an effective way of involving reluctant pupils, as well as a means of showing understanding of new vocabulary. When introducing instructions - '*Look! Listen! Stand up! Show me! Sit down! Open your books!*' - great fun can be had in devising and carrying out mimes to fit these expressions. Sports, hobbies and animals are some of the other vocabulary areas which lend themselves well to miming.

- Performing simple radio plays, jingles or weather forecasts. These can be taped with the addition of sound effects and music.

Of course, several of these activities require space if they are to be successful and, not least of all, safe. It may be difficult to organise them in a classroom and it is worth considering using the school hall or playground.

PUPPETS

Primary school children generally like watching and creating puppet shows. Using puppets in the foreign language classroom can bring a new dimension to lessons. They are a colourful and enjoyable way to introduce unknown vocabulary and structures, and they give the pupils the opportunity to handle something concrete while they assimilate the new language.

Pupils who are generally shy or inhibited can be encouraged to participate by 'speaking through' a puppet. If a mistake is made, it is the puppet who has made the error, not the pupil.

Puppets can be used in a variety of ways. For example, each pupil prepares a few phrases about her or his puppet and presents them to the class. The puppet can be given a name, age, birthday, likes and dislikes, etc. They can also be used in pair work, with pupils developing a short dialogue between their puppets. This can be extended to groups producing puppet plays with familiar settings, such as the café or the market, as well as more creative ones such as on another planet.

The teacher can provide the puppets, the children can bring in their own or they can make them as part of a classroom activity. However, it is important that the initial presentation of the puppets by the teacher is done in an enjoyable and relaxed manner. The teacher sets the tone in the classroom. If he or she enjoys using the puppets, the pupils will accept and use them more readily.

STORY TELLING

Telling simple stories in the foreign language is an enjoyable and motivating way of developing pupils' skills. These stories can be shared with a class purely for pleasure or they can be used to provide a range of activities.

The stories may be traditional fairy tales or modern ones such as *Bernard et le monstre* better known here as *Not now Bernard*. They may originate from a particular country, such as *The Pied Piper of Hamlin* and *Hansel and Gretel*, or they may be taken from many of the bilingual story books now available in this country. Primary teachers are often expert at writing and adapting stories themselves, and if a school is lucky enough to have a parent or parents who are native speakers, this is one of many areas where their skills and knowledge are extremely valuable. If this particular 'resource' is not available, a local secondary school may be able - with plenty of advance warning - to lend their Foreign Language Assistant to assist with such activities.

A well known fairy tale, such as *Goldilocks*, can be the vehicle to practise the language needed to talk about family members, physical descriptions and simple adjectives. Once children are familiar with the language they can produce their own scripts and perform them in groups. Alternatively, they can write a simplified version and illustrate it in a storyboard or cartoon format. Teachers may wish to give their pupils a muddled version of the story to re-order or some of the text with words missing to be filled in, with or without support.

PRACTICAL ACTIVITIES

One of our main objectives is to 'involve pupils in active learning', and one of the most effective ways of doing this is to use the foreign language to make real objects. To be able to carry out such tasks the pupils will have to listen to or read the instructions and be able to ask for help if necessary. If the foreign language is used in this way, it will give a true purpose to the pupils' learning. Many of these tasks involve other areas of the curriculum, such as maths, technology, design. They may also necessitate group and pair work, and therefore foster skills of interaction and co-operation between the children. Primary school teachers will already have many ideas for and experience of practical activities. The following suggestions are tried and tested:

- **Making vocabulary mobiles**. Not only are these a useful means of support, they are also attractive to display. They do not necessarily have to include a 2D model, they can simply include the useful phrases for classroom language: *'How do you say that in...?' 'I have forgotten.' 'Open your books.'*

- **Designing and making cards**. These can be for birthdays, Christmas, New Year, Mother's day, Easter etc, with the appropriate message.

- **Making masks**. These can be made using paper plates or card. The pupils will need to know the words for glue, scissors, pencils and so on. The finished articles can be used for display with the addition of written descriptions, or in role-play to help the children put on another character.

- **Cooking**. Given the restrictions of a 'normal' classroom, this does not have to be as difficult as it may sound! 'Cooking' can be anything from making a snack or a drink to decorating a chocolate log. If lack of facilities prevent as much pupil participation as one would like, a teacher demonstration followed by tasting is a popular option. The recipes can always be given for 'homework' and many pupils are keen to bring in the fruits of their labours. Some schools have focused their foreign language work around preparing a meal typical of the country whose language they are learning. Activities have included making paper place mats and printing on them using potatoes and other vegetables, making clay vases to decorate the meal tables and the paper flowers to go in them and designing and printing menus using IT. All this has been achieved using the target language.

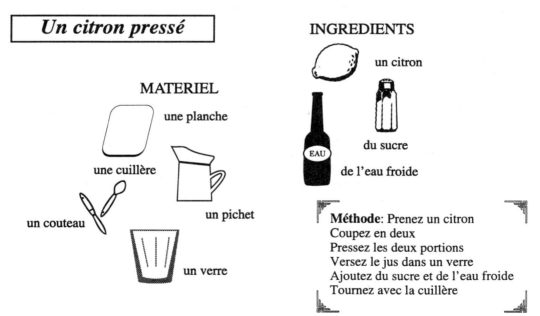

Un citron pressé

MATERIEL
une planche
une cuillère
un couteau
un pichet
un verre

INGREDIENTS
un citron
du sucre
de l'eau froide
EAU

Méthode: Prenez un citron
Coupez en deux
Pressez les deux portions
Versez le jus dans un verre
Ajoutez du sucre et de l'eau froide
Tournez avec la cuillère

Jeu de découpage

Découpez-moi en seize morceaux et essayez de me reconstituer.
Servez-vous de ceci comme modèle.

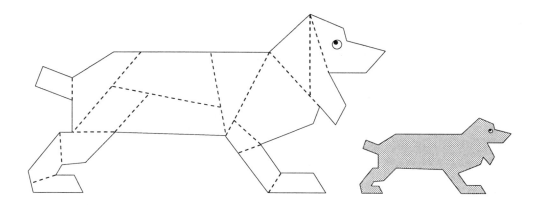

There are many other practical activities which lend themselves to early foreign language learning. They include the following:

- designing posters
- producing a display
- making simple books
- making games, i.e. card or board games
- making puppets
- making decorations
- illustrating a story
- producing a cartoon sequence
- making a 'fortune teller'
- constructing models of houses, shops, villages
- designing menus
- making weather or birthday charts
- drawing town plans or maps
- designing a fantasy island or planet
- making a die or a spinner to practise numbers, colours etc
- producing puzzles, wordsearches, crosswords.

4   Teaching in the target language

Throughout this book we have almost taken it for granted that primary teachers, whether non-specialists or language graduates, will endeavour to teach most of each lesson in the foreign language, the 'target' language. This is the ideal to strive for, but the reality of the classroom is not as simple as that. Very few primary teachers are language graduates and fewer and fewer are being offered access to a foreign language option as part of B.Ed courses in ITE. It is unrealistic to expect non-graduates in a foreign language to have anything approaching native speaker fluency - indeed this is rarely achieved by secondary teachers who are language graduates! It is important to realise, however, that you do not have to be a linguistic genius to teach a foreign language successfully to primary children. As Keith Sharpe said, '*Primary French tends to be more primary than French*' (Sharpe, Language Learning Journal, 1993) - and all those brave Scottish teachers who took part in the Pilot Project will confirm this. What you do need to do, however, is to be honest with yourself about your linguistic strengths and weaknesses.

TAKING STOCK OF YOUR LANGUAGE SKILLS

What should you be asking yourself?

- Have I been to the foreign country recently?
- Is my knowledge of the language reasonably up to date?
- Could I still 'get by' in the foreign country?
- Is my pronunciation and intonation reasonably accurate? How do I check this?
- Do I have access to a native speaker or language specialist colleague who might help?
- Do I have access to any adult level self-tuition materials to refresh my knowledge (e.g. BBC or other published language packs)?
- Do I have access to any primary level materials that would help me in the classroom (e.g. *Pilote, Trampoline, Wer?Wie? Was?*)?
- Is there any possibility of team teaching with a more confident colleague?
- Do I have any access to appropriate in-service training in my area?
- Are there any local adult education classes to brush up my language?
- Do I have a good up-to-date bilingual dictionary (e.g. Collins/Robert, Harrap, Usborne Picture dictionaries)?

Obviously it would be just as foolish to assume that **anyone** can teach a foreign language at the drop of a hat as it would for music, science or technology; but a combination of enthusiasm, hard work and common sense can go a long way, provided that there is some additional linguistic support and expertise close at hand. Many of the Scottish primary teachers, for example, started the Pilot Project in 1989 with the linguistic support of peripatetic secondary teachers who visited twice a week to teach the keynote lessons. These were progressively followed up by the class teachers, who in many cases eventually took over responsibility for the language lessons as their confidence grew.

PLANNING YOUR TARGET LANGUAGE STRATEGIES

Even with a relatively modest command of a language you **can** sustain lessons in the target language if:

- you plan your lessons very carefully and script the target language (TL) you expect to use;
- you relax with your class and enjoy yourself in the TL;
- you are brave and not afraid to make mistakes (**all** language teachers make mistakes with genders, word order, verb endings, etc!);
- you stick to a limited repertoire of simple phrases and sentences which you re-use each week (e.g. class routines, instructions, questions, explanations of activities, games);
- you do not attempt to explain everything in words;
- you use plenty of mime, gesture, facial expressions, body language (remember the French, Italians and Spaniards always talk with their hands and faces!);
- you use plenty of visual cues - pictures, flashcards, OHP drawings, realia, puppets, soft animals;
- you make regular use of audio and video cassettes, songs and games;
- you plan the language of your lesson as well as the content - i.e. you script what you will say and also what the children will need to say;
- you consciously teach the children 'survival language' - e.g. *'I don't understand; may I go to the toilet please; I haven't got a pen; can I borrow a pencil please?'*;
- you encourage the use of picture dictionaries from the outset;
- you allow the children to learn from their - and your - mistakes;
- you make contact with a native speaker (FLA, secondary colleague, or parent) as your linguistic 'consultant';
- you are not 'purist' about doing everything in the target language, when some things (e.g. explanations of how language works, unusual words) can be more quickly and effectively dealt with in English;
- you make a real effort to immerse yourself as often as possible in the sounds and culture of the foreign language out of school hours - cassettes or foreign radio stations in the car, evening classes, home videos, reading magazines and newspapers, holidays abroad...

In conclusion, we would like to emphasise that we all have a great deal yet to learn about how young children acquire a second language - no two children appear to learn in exactly the same way. It seems to us sensible to be flexible and open-minded in our methodology and much of what we do in the classroom will inevitably be a process of trial and error. However, we can learn a lot from the teachers of English as a foreign language in the rest of Europe, as well as from the experiments of Scottish primary teachers. There are many interesting and patently successful ideas in the SCOPE/SOED videos which may inspire teachers to try out similar activities.

Classroom practice in the pilot phase of the Scottish Primary Project shows distinct echoes of the longstanding successes in Canadian and Australian primary schools, where 'partial immersion' experiments over twenty years have proved that large parts of the normal primary curriculum can be successfully taught through the medium of a foreign language. How far we in the UK can begin to move in this direction will depend very much on the linguistic expertise, the confidence, and the imagination of classroom teachers - and the quality of the resources and in-service training available. For the present we should perhaps simply ask ourselves whether the traditional approach to foreign language learning as discrete lessons taught by a 'specialist' could eventually be replaced by a more integrated, cross-curricular approach which places the class teacher in the central role of linking foreign language activities to the daily routines and the broadly planned topic work of the class. We should watch closely developments in Scottish primary schools in the next few years and learn from their experience.

We hope that many more primary teachers who are not necessarily language 'specialists' will be encouraged to take the plunge to brush up their language skills and broaden the horizons of their pupils by introducing them to the language and the culture of a foreign country.

With a little courage, imagination, and some practical support from your headteacher - and perhaps some native speakers in the local community - it is surprising what can be achieved. Learning a new language can and should be fun - for the children and the teacher! Above all, if we are going to teach languages to young children, we must do it well or not at all.

We hope that you will have found food for thought in this book and that it will spur you into action. We wish you and your pupils every enjoyment and success!

Appendix 1: primary languages projects

In the last few years several important projects have been set up in Scotland and England.

The major **Scottish Primary Project** was piloted in selected areas from 1989 with substantial government funding for four years. Such was the resounding success and the impact of this project that it has received major government funding through the SOED to provide a substantial linguistic/methodological retraining package for teachers in all Scottish primary schools, starting in 1994. This project has also led to the production of some excellent SOED videos recording primary children's confident performance in German, French, Italian and Spanish. These children demonstrate what a wide variety of topics can be tackled in primary schools and what enormous satisfaction and sheer pleasure they get from performing in a new language. (SOED: *Foreign languages in the primary school*, three videos + viewing guide, SCOPE, 1994).

On a much smaller scale a few English LEAs have funded primary languages projects with similar aims: to retrain existing primary class teachers to teach one year of a foreign language to beginners.

Kent has so far funded the retraining of over 100 teachers to teach French, Spanish or Portuguese to children in Year 6 and has recently published a high quality French learning pack, *Pilote*, which provides non-specialist teachers with a year's classroom support materials. The pack contains three videos, teachers notes and materials, and is available from Language Centre Publications, Leamington.

Since 1993 **Surrey** and **Richmond** have provided similar in-service training courses for a limited number of primary teachers, combining linguistic refreshment with methodology. Surrey has published *Guidelines for EFLL* (1994). Richmond has published a French teaching resource pack, *C'est facile comme 'Bonjour'!* (1994).

In 1993 pilot projects in primary German were set up in **Cornwall** and **West Sussex** with the support of the Goethe Institute and these have so far proved very successful. German has been introduced alongside French in Years 5 + 6.

In addition to these LEA initiatives there have been interesting developments recently in Northern Ireland and in many individual schools in London and the rest of England and Wales, who have launched their own experiments in Italian, Spanish, and community languages - as well as French.

Appendix 2: resources

In a short book of this nature it is not possible to list all the currently available resources. Those selected are some of the most interesting and valuable commercially produced resources that teachers in primary schools have used and recommended. They are listed by language and most likely age group: 4-7/ 8-10.

For a more comprehensive list refer to the CILT Information Sheets: *Early language learning: a guide for parents* (OL23), *French for young beginners: teaching materials* (52), *German for young beginners: teaching materials* (53), *Italian materials for young beginners* (93), *Spanish materials for young beginners* (94), *Teaching languages to young beginners: reports and guides* (55).

Resources for French (4-7)

Bruzzone C, *Just for Kids* (Berlitz, 1992)
Handbook + 3 cassettes

Delbende J-C and V Heuze, *Le français en chantant* (Didier/European Schoolbooks, 1992)
Teacher's book, pupil book, cassette

Deshmulch C, *Allez France! activity repro-master pack* (European Schoolbooks, 1993)
200 photocopiable resources

Kay J, *Un kilo de chansons* (Mary Glasgow Publications, 1978)
Cassette of 12 songs + lyrics + teacher's notes

Meyer-Dreux S, *Le petit trampoline* (CLE International/European Schoolbooks, 1994)
Pupil's book, teacher's book, 2 cassettes

Nyburg A, *French for fun* (Harrap, 1991)
Book + cassette

Nyburg A, *Further French for fun* (Harrap, 1991)
Book + cassette

Paccagnino C and M-L Poletti, *Kangourou* (Level 1) (Hachette, 1991)
Teacher's book, pupil workbook, posters, figurines

French (8 -10)

BBC, *Le Club* (BBC Education, 1994)
10 radio programmes, teacher's notes

Clarke A, Burrows and others, *Aventures* (Lincolnwood NTC, 1990)
Song book + teacher's guide + 3 cassettes
Pupil book, workbook, teacher's book

Sussex County Council, *Salut la France* (Simon & Schuster, 1989)
Teacher's book, resource pack, 3 workbooks, cassette

Kent Primary French Project, *Pilote* (KETV, 1992)
3 part video-based course for non-specialist primary teachers. Teacher's notes, pupil materials, INSET video

Idées pratiques pour la classe de français (Mary Glasgow Publications, 1991)

Le Hellaye C and D Barzotti, *Farandole* (Hatier/Didier, 1992)
Pupil book, workbook, teacher's book, 2 cassettes

Allons (Mary Glasgow Magazines)
Illustrated magazine + cassette

Meyer-Dreux S and others, *Trampoline* (CLE International, 1991-)
Pupil book, workbook, teachers's guide, 4 cassettes

Muffin (series) (Muffin Canada, 1986-1989)
Cassettes + songbooks. Series includes '*Comment ça va?*' and *Quand tu seras grand*

Voilà! (ELI Magazines)

German (5 - 7)

Bruzzone C, *German just for kids* (Berlitz, 1992)
Workbook, 3 cassettes

Gobel H et al, *Du und ich* (Langenscheidt, 1983)
Teacher's handbook, songbook, media folder - games, worksheets, picture cards

Güsti GR and F Merci, *Alle Affen und Giraffen* (Verlag für Deutsch, 1993)
Song cassette + songbook

Liederkiste (European Schoolbooks)
Song cassette

Nyburg A, *German for fun* (Chambers Harrap, 1991)
Book + cassette

German (8 - 10)

Augustin V and others, *Aurelia 1* (Langenscheidt, 1994)
Pupil book, workbook, 2 cassettes, OHTs

Das Kinder-Lieder-Buch (European Schoolbooks)
Traditional Children's Songs

Fertig... Los! (ELI Magazines)
Magazine featuring cartoon strips/games

Huckepack (Klett)
Teacher resource book, handbook, cassette

Praktische Ideen für den Deutschunterricht (Mary Glasgow Publications, 1991)

Rissel, Rassel, Russel (European Schoolbooks)
Rhymes, puzzles, etc

Seeger H and T Vieth, *Wer? Wie? Was?* (Gilde Buchhandlung Carl Kayser, 1989-)
Pupil book, workbook, teacher's book, 2 cassettes, glove puppet, 5 readers. (See also Wahl M, *Lieder machen Spaß*.)

Wahl M, *Lieder machen Spaß* (Gilde Buchhandlung Carl Kayser, 1993)
Songbook + cassette to support *Wer? Wie? Was?* (see above)

Italian (8 -10)

Avanti (European Schoolbooks)
Pupil book, teacher's book, 4 cassettes,
workbook, 4 readers

Azzuro: il mensile per tuo italiano (ELI
Magazines)

Bruzzone C, *Italian just for kids* (Berlitz,
1992)
Workbook, 3 cassettes

Idee pratiche per leziono d'italiano
(Mary Glasgow Publications, 1991)

Spanish (8 - 10)

Bruzzone C, *Spanish just for kids* (Berlitz,
1992)
Workbook, 3 cassettes

Ideas practicas para la classe de español
(Mary Glasgow Publications, 1992)

Juegos faciles (LCP, 1994)
Photocopiable word games + activities

¿Que tal? (Mary Glasgow Magazines)

Vamos! (ELI Magazines)

Wood S, *Spanish for fun* (Chambers
Harrap, 1991)
Workbook and cassette

Bibliography

De Silva J and P Satchwell, *Guidelines for early foreign language learning in primary schools* (Surrey CC, 1994)

Fernandez S, *Room for two: a study of bilingual education at Bayswater South Primary School* (Australia: NLLIA, 1992)

First steps to language learning: CILT Conference report (CILT, May 1994)

Halliwell S and B Jones, *On target: teaching in the target language* (CILT, 1991)

Hawkins E, *Modern languages in the curriculum*, (CUP, 1981)

Johnson P, *A book of one's own* (Hodder & Stoughton, 1991)

Johnstone R (ed), *Making a start! Modern languages in the primary classroom* (CILT, 1995)

Learning and teaching: French for primary schools (SCOPE, 1994)
Video + teacher support notes + class activities pack *Education*

Learning and teaching: German for primary schools (SCOPE, 1994)
Video + Teacher support notes + class activities pack *Education*

Low L, J Duffield, S Brown and R Johnstone, *Evaluating foreign languages in primary schools* (SCILT, 1993)

'Modern foreign languages in primary schools' in *Newsletter 1* (SCILT, 1994)

Modern languages in the primary school (SOED SCOPE, 1994)
3 videos + viewing guide *Education*

Pilote (KETV, 1994)
3 teaching videos + teacher's notes + 1 INSET video

Sharpe K, 'Communication, culture, context, confidence: the four Cs of primary modern language teaching' in *Language Learning Journal*, no. 6 (ALL, Sept. 1992)